GW00499735

Haiku From The Asylum

DAVID ROLLINS

ISBN:1999876539
ISBN-13:9781999876531

FIRST EDITION

GREEN CAT BOOKS

www.green-cat.co/books

David Rollins

INTRODUCTION

Haiku are Japanese poetry form, consisting of 3 lines, and a syllable count of 5-7-5. They should reflect the now, and ideally the first two lines should converge on the third conclusive line.

These are my experiences of living as a service user in a mental health ward in Leicester, the first written about a month after entry and the last either after a year, a discharge or death.

Although I was tempted to group them into similar themes, I felt they were far more powerful in the order they were written, showing both hope and despair as they arise. There are inevitably more haiku in moments of despair, as (along with a significant number of poets, I suspect) those are the times when I emote more, and so write more. That said, I hope that you do not find the collection depressing, but thought provoking. All names except my own have been changed.

I present to you

Haiku From The Asylum

By David Rollins

ACKNOWLEDGMENTS

To Alison who started me back on Haiku
To Lydia who inspired me to keep writing
To Beth who proof read my first manuscript
To Charlotte who p.a'd for me when I needed it
To Lisa who took the risk of publishing me
To Talmon and Jared always.

**********Pre-Mental Health Ward And Why**********

(July)

1

It turns out I died

and the bastards brought me back.

I wish they hadn't

2

A wheelchair entry

in the middle of the night

my first asylum

3

I expect chaos,

screaming, violence and cuckoos

but it's just a ward

4

Maybe this will help

since death appears to deny me,

should I hope or not?

********* July...Early Thoughts*************

5

The darkness taunts me,

the tablets are just causing

a waking nightmare.

6

I planned my own death,

instead I'm in the Bradgate,

but the nurse is hot.

7

The psychiatrist

is intrigued by my thinking.

We start to bargain.

8

They think I don't care,

I do, and that's the problem,

it makes me angry

*************My First Few Friends In Here************

9

Dan talks all the time,

words running into the next

till no one listens.

10

Alan cries a bit

but mostly he laughs a lot

a strange sound in here

11

Sat in writing class

and saw Debbie sitting there,

and thought, wow, just wow.

12

Young woman, Sandy,

Enjoys smoking cigarettes

They don't calm her down

13

I lie here thinking

about life on the outside,

where I don't fit in.

***** Observations On Staff After A Few Weeks*****

14

The people in here

Are like fragments of myself

I'm that fucked up now

15

Beautiful Helen

in her nurse's uniform.

She thinks she's ugly

16

Sara sits and chats,

the daughter I never had,

another regret.

17

Doctor Malla sits

in the ward round and listens,

he understands me.

**********A Month In, Settling Into Routines********
(August)

18

I'm allowed off ward

The idea horrifies me

I write more Haiku

19

The hoover is loud

when you try to catch the sleep

that you lost last night

20

There are drugs in here

Cannabis is smuggled in

for those who need it.

21

The trolley man comes.

Papers and chocolate abound,

Highlight of each day

22

The food is awful,

and at fifty pence per meal

you'd have to be mad.

***************A Few New Patients**************

23

He talks to himself

then kicks and punches the air.

Schizophrenic Tom

24

Al barely whispers,

He won't even eat or drink.

Vulnerable in here

25

I saw you light up

then throw dog-ends on the grass...

You selfish Bastards.

26

Tom sells drugs in here,

he has cancer and coughs up,

he hasn't got long.

27

I share a room now.

Heavy breathing over there,

I hope it's just sleep

28

Jack has been discharged,

his tablets have been delayed

impotent raging.

**************Starting To Get Better***************

29

First day out in town,

Nando's with Ivy and Tal,

It's scary out here

30

Dairy Milk, new jeans

Do nothing to calm me down

I need to return

*****************Ward Life****************

31

The best food in here,

the one that we all desire...

Chocolate, white, dark, milk.

32

Extremely frightened

Mahmoud doesn't speak English.

No interpreters!

33

One bookcase, one desk,

a table, eight comfy chairs,

a pleasant ward lounge.

34

Strolling in pj's,

Liam's mohican and abs

contrasts his kindness.

35

The clock moves slowly.

Weekends, no activities.

Waiting for nothing.

36

Giving up on sleep,

The lounge is where we wander

until the ward wakes.

37

Group chat on the grass,

men and women talking sex.

God I love it here.

********* A Brief Relapse Into Introspection**********

38

I'm on self-destruct

thoughts running around my head.

Suicidal me

39

It's visiting time,

I don't know who's visiting.

They all belong here.

40

Night staff on a break,

have to wait an hour for meds...

Then I get angry.

41

Too annoyed to sleep.

Pulling the sheet over me.

Escaping the world

42

Peter, nurse in charge,

one of the more helpful ones.

An all-round good guy.

43

Support worker Josh

looks at me with his owl eyes,

Blinking nervously

*****************Relationships In Here***************

44

She likes me, she thinks,

(of all the places to meet),

I like her, I think.

45

Beautiful Debbie,

won't you come out to dinner

with me one evening?

46

Talking, laughter, noise

the pool balls hit by the cue.

All Asylum sounds

47

Some of the old guys

tell of former asylums.

I guess I'm lucky.

48

New meds for sleeping,

at last I can sleep soundly.

Good night everybody

49

Katy sits, chats with us,

Friendly and approachable

We all like Katy.

50

There's two crowds in here,

the quiet indoor readers,

then there's the smokers.

51

Strange agency staff,

Don't know them and don't trust them,

Who the fuck are they?

52

Staff make tea for staff.

Users make tea for users.

We live separate lives

53

Green walls and brown doors,

too many fluorescent lights.

I feel like my ward.

54

Bloody night workers

keep waking us up again,

constantly talking.

55

Sue, the new inmate,

young, friendly, vulnerable.

Shouldn't be in here.

*************Good Days And Bad Days*************

56

Not suicidal!

Meds and therapy working.

I am almost fixed

57

The Pole speaks English

but keeps on speaking Polish.

Annoying woman!

58

I was doing well.

Today I feel so pissed off,

and I don't know why.

59

There is too much noise

that it's so overwhelming.

I just want silence.

********** I Don't Know Who I Am Any More*********

60

If I start to hope

I risk being frustrated

Or much worse, violent

61

I went out today,

it all felt so chaotic.

I can't live out there.

62

Talking one to one,

I think, is underrated.

It helps me a lot

63

I keep telling them

why I want to take my life.

They just don't get it.

64

Suicide because

the past... and the present are

equally to blame.

65

Can anyone live

with who they are becoming?

Maybe, but I can't

66

Sunday evening.

My abuse a mere shadow.

I'd rather be dead.

67

Damn the student nurse

not listening to what I said,

now I'm stuck on ward.

************ Getting Angrier Not Better**********

68

It's quiet sat here.

Inevitably a shout,

now it's not quiet.

69

Trembling and headaches.

Medication makes me worse.

Everyone go away.

70

The phone room is free

so I ask to use it, but

the nurse just walks away.

71

I was doing well

Today I hate Ashby ward

It's hurting my head

72

I've been here two months.

I now have less visitors,

Because shit happens

73

Anger and tiredness

between them control my mind

and fuel my despair.

74

Filling in a form

so I can have a sandwich!

I think, 'what the fuck'?

75

I want ham salad.

They can do ham OR salad.

Institutional

76

I feel more helpless

The longer I stay in here

The rules are stupid

77

I don't want to stay

but then I don't want to leave.

I am in limbo

******Observations At The End Of Month Two*******

78

Smokers in the yard

cough up outside my bedroom.

I hate my new room

79

Debs, feisty and cute,

we made friends that first evening.

Will we stay in touch?

80

There is SO much noise.

I decide to perforate

My ear with a stick

81

Becca shouts and bangs,

wrecking the user kitchen.

It doesn't take long.

82

I read the papers.

Out there seems irrelevant.

Other people's lives.

********** I Can't Think Clearly**********

83

Moved into a dorm

as though I were just cattle

with no say at all.

84

Sharing a bedroom

will make friends of enemies,

and vice versa.

85

Four other in mates

Take it in turns with snoring

It's taking the piss

86

Two hours of listening

And failing to get to sleep

I finally snap

87

I grab my bedding

Dragging it to a bathroom

And get some shut eye

88

A half hour later

The staff do their routine checks

And find I'm not there

89

They search frantically

Eventually finding me

Asleep by a sink

90

They kept on at me

Citing health and safety rules

I just ignored them

91

Every few minutes

The nurse would come and argue

So I couldn't sleep

92

Eventually

He goaded me to grab him

And backed out the door

93

I was surrounded

There were six more big men

I had been set up

94

Arms and legs restrained

I head butted two of them

Before I was stopped

95

Off to 'seclusion'

The new name for rubber room

Where I spend the night

96

'What's that fucking noise?'

It's the ventilation fan

They won't turn it off

97

The following day

The psych wanted to see me

To discuss last night

98

My anger was caused

by Serotonin Syndrome.

So it wasn't me

99

All I want is sleep,

meds made me over-react

and someone got hurt.

100

They say it's the meds.

I wonder where the meds end

and David begins.

101

 Becca likes my shirts,

The slogans make us both laugh.

Lunatic humour.

******Can Think A Bit Now, More Reflections*******

102

Can't see a future,

being dead is easier.

How can I function?

103

Planning going home,

my care plan says I have to.

Lots to think about

104

Fighting one by one,

as though we take it in turns.

To attack the guards

105

Lucy, student nurse,

was nervous, now confident.

She'll do well... maybe.

Now I've Had Enough.. Passive Resistance

106

I'm now on new meds

Staff, wards, meds make me feel worse,

I retreat inwards.

107

It felt safe in here,

now I don't know what to think.

Can they be trusted?

108

I tried to fix me,

I let them try to fix me,

and now... I'm not fixed.

109

Going back out there

may not be the best idea,

neither is staying.

110

The night staff in here

don't like us disturbing them.

They sleep, but we don't

111

Can't fault the day staff,

Mostly I find them friendly

And approachable

**************More Staff**************

112

Ian, tall, young, blond

Inmates call him cutie pie,

Its hysterical

113

My named nurse, Charlie

A big man with a kind heart

and too much to do.

114

Nurse Mai is useless,

unless CQC are here...

Then she is helpful.

115

Ward manager, Anne,

firm, fair, not to be messed with.

Strong and silent type.

116

Simon, uses the

Excuse of health and safety

To avoid working

117

Adam is quiet,

an unsung force of nature.

There's peace on his watch.

**********Back On The Right Track Again**********

118

Communication,

hard enough with mental health,

glad I speak English.

119

Dizzy all the time.

No one wants to get the doc,

It's next shifts problem.

120

Suicide Sundays.

Will today be one or not?

I don't really care.

121

In here I exist,

not getting better or worse

and never leaving.

122

Who remembers me?

Who thinks I'm a lunatic?

Who cares anyway?

123

The novelty gone.

Week one, thirteen visitors,

week twelve, only three.

David Rollins

124

Seven guys sat round

chatting football and women

and then Sharif farts

125

Charlotte does not speak

friendly, beautiful eyes mock.

As she smiles at me

126

For bad bathroom smells

the worst is not from shit, it's

self induced vomit.

127

Reading quietly.

then someone starts playing pool

I leave, angrily.

Given Up Caring, Not Getting Better, Getting Worse

128

Today I moved wards

From Ashby to Watermead.

Ancient to modern.

129

Its goodbye dorm rooms

Now I have a private room

Now I might get sleep

130

I am woken up

All through the night by the staff

Switching on the lights.

131

They reduced my meds

without telling me so now

I'm in pain again.

132

How do I get out

without lying to them all?

Pretending I'm sane

133

Feeling really bleak

Just passing the days away

More suicide thoughts

134

Some staff seem to think

that they can talk down to us

as though we're stupid.

135

Liquorice allsorts

at two ten in the morning.

Insomnia snacks

136

Staff must surely know

sleeplessness is depressive.

Yet they're so noisy.

***********More Introspection***********

137

Weekly psych meeting

Yet another plan for me

But nothing's working

138

Nothing beyond now,

can't think about tomorrow.

I can't take it in.

139

People on this ward

Might have been more likeable

Were I not depressed

140

It's about balance.

Pros and cons fight for my life

but what should I weigh?

141

Rooted in the past

my thoughts go back to abuse.

Nothing I could do.

142

I can't seem to die,

so must work out what I want,

or just keep trying.

143

I think my care plan

is pick a card, any card

and then put it back.

144

Our hands in pockets

we walk all around the ward,

but there's nothing new.

**********Asylum Conversations**********

145

"David, you OK?"

"If I was OK", I say,

"I wouldn't be here."

146

'Discharge or section',

I propose, and see their eyes,

sad and resolute.

147

'Well, how about this, '

they try, frustrated again

I nod, and they smile

148

'You're intelligent'.

'If I was', I then reply,

'then I would be dead'

*********A Resolution Once Again*************

149

Hoping I will die

I look at my inmate friends

and feel affection

150

I don't know how yet,

something will present itself

when the time is right

********New Ideas Provided*********

151

I love this bedroom

It's like sound proofing all night

I might get some sleep

152

A new painkiller?

Oh... This one's going to work!

I won't hold my breath

153

Tchaikovsky music

makes writing poetry easy

my iPad does both

154

My landlord has said

he'll make changes to my flat

so I can move back.

155

Hope/cynicism

run side by side in my head.

I'll just wait and see

*****Some Of My Suicide Reasons ********

156

I have lots of friends

But I just didn't see it

A character flaw?

157

Homo Sapian swarm

is destroying this planet,

and I'm just as bad.

158

I have no soul mate.

What does mine even look like?

Awful loneliness.

159

Every bloody month

my wages just disappeared.

Can't stay out of debt.

160

Why is everything

much harder than it should be?

It's Fucking jobsworths.

161

A conversation...

"We all have to live with it"

'No... I don't', I say.

162

I have a t shirt

' common sense is so rare...it's

a superpower.'

163

On minimum wage,

making money for the rich

day in and day out.

164

No God, no purpose

I've got existential angst....

A need to find out.

165

To hate who you are.

To know how others see you.

Who could live with that?

***********Moved To A New Ward***********

166

Lots of differences,

but you never really know

until things kick off.

167

Its all going well

The ward is clean and airy,

but it's the same food.

168

The staff seem cheerful.

This new glass and metal ward

Has much more sunlight

******** Some New People******

169

Sarah has hamsters

and a lovely heart and smile,

my new favourite nurse.

170

Kal showed me around,

nothing was too much trouble,

the kind Asian nurse.

Some Things Change And Some Things Don't

171

It's now been 3 months.

I came in summer, but now

I need winter clothes.

172

When will I leave here?

I still want to take my life,

So... maybe never.

173

Creative writing,

Lee shows me some new ideas

while soft music plays.

174

The new psych is vague

not answering my questions.

What is he hiding?

175

Doctor S suggests

that I may have a future,

I just don't see it.

176

It's taken a while.

Now they start to ask themselves

if I'm not depressed.

177

Plans to meet a friend.

She cancelled on me AGAIN.

A friend? I now ask.

***** Noises On A Quiet Ward********

178

Watching the tv,

then people come in chatting,

every single time.

179

Banging bedroom doors

Is alright during the day,

but thoughtless at night.

180

I have two ears, but

more than one person talking

at once hurts my head.

******* Day To Day Living*******

181

Punjabi wedding

so I'm out for one whole day.

Even though I'm scared.

182

Days come and days go,

I lie on my bed reading

in perfect silence.

183

Lavender oil

as well as medication.

Got a good night's sleep.

184

I'm allowed off ward,

So I visit my old flat

But, now it feels strange.

******A New Hope?*******

185

Junior psych Sheila

focused on the pain symptom.

She had an idea.

186

One pain test later

And a new diagnosis

Fibromyalgia

*****Random Stuff********

187

Pain and sleeplessness,

headache, noise intolerance...

So far it all fits

188

Good news or bad news?

Does it mean I'm not insane?

No, probably not.

189

Last night I was God

and then I was fierce lightning.

Diazepam dreams

190

FDL group stuff.

The only interesting thing

was the almost fight

191

My whole body hurts

and once again I'm thinking

I'm better off dead

192

The usual slop

Instead a small lie gets me

Caribbean food

193

Lots of people here,

but nobody to talk to.

Pointlessness is hell.

194

My arms feel like lead,

I can't be bothered to think,

I'm just existing

********Leaving********

195

Tried to get discharged,

took all day to get nowhere.

I'm now exhausted.

196

Going in circles.

If I leave I'll be in debt

I think about death.

197

Don't want to stay here,

and don't want to live out there...

So I do nothing.

*******November*******

198

A shit asylum

That doesn't even have ghosts.

An urban myth-take

199

"You're all gonna die",

shouts an inmate to us all

as we eat breakfast.

******Damp Flats And Colds*******

200

Back home for one night.

What to pack for overnight?

My confidence gone.

201

I stayed for one night

in a flat that was once mine.

Now it feels all wrong.

202

My flat is too damp,

I feel miserable and cold.

I long to go back.

203

Now I've caught a cold.

Lemsips and Olbas oil.

Could my life get worse?

204

I feel safe on ward.

I'm just so cold and tired,

so I lie here, numb.

205

My mind is so small.

Once it included a god

Now there's just my thoughts.

206

A head full of cold.

A finger and a touchscreen

A brain of Haiku

207

Marina has a

onesie that looks like a bear..

Her bi-polar bear

*******My Writing Mentors********

208

My friends, the poets,

Pink haired woman pouring tea.

While our pens are poised.

209

In the writing group

Caroline cheerfully draws

feelings into words

*******Being Discharged... Maybe*****

210

The psych says I'm fine

with the support that I'll have.

Next Wednesday I leave

211

I've told lots of friends

I am being discharged soon.

A few are worried.

212

Looking forward to

cooking, drinking, meeting friends...

Things I used to do.

213

Do they need the bed?

Or else this doesn't make sense.

My discharge worries.

214

Saw an ex patient

dishevelled in town today.

Did they need his bed?

215

Free to return home

no saner than when I left.

Suicidal me

216

Decision day looms

and I find that I don't care.

Live/die... Not my choice.

217

I brought a giraffe,

a fluffy one for my sons

twentieth birthday.

218

My flat stinks of damp,

Phased return makes me wonder.

Can I live back here?

*******All Change Again*******

219

I'm going insane.

They've moved my discharge date back

without a ward round.

220

Another ward round...

They tell me I will move wards

as they need this bed.

221

Housing benefit

finally came through today.

Good news at long last.

222

My new ward... Aston.

They promised a single room.

They lied yet again.

223

Not expecting sleep.

Three more inmates, one bedroom.

Suicidal thoughts.

224

A ward of old men,

yet somehow I feel at home..

That's not a good thing.

225

Staff ask 'who are you?'

I tell them, and then rudely

they don't tell me theirs.

226

My chocolate stolen

A room-mate is a tea leaf,

and the staff just shrug.

227

I see more reasons

from institutional life

to try suicide.

228

It's that kind of day

when small things matter, like the

jeans zip not working.

229

The thief said sorry

after I made it clear that

I knew it was him.

230

Cooks said they'd save lunch

for when I got back on ward.

They forgot... Again

****Finally Being Discharged After 4 Months****

231

Back to this again...

Will I stay or should I go?

The ward psych decides.

232

One ward round later

the psych decides I'm going.

Now so much to do.

233

Without the Ipad

replacing my memory

I'd have no idea.

234

Glad I'm going home,

but already so tired.

Fibro-fatigue strikes.

235

Shopping and cleaning

occupy my every thought

and I'm panicking.

236

I wear mental health

as a shield protecting me

from a hostile world.

237

A weekend at home

tidying and cleaning up

four months of absence.

238

An afternoon sleep

ruined by next door's music.

Hello my old life.

239

Back on ward again

trying to watch the tv

but there's so much noise

240

Almost left the ward,

but the meds haven't arrived

so sleeping over.

241

Couldn't make it up.

The bloody pharmacy took

Twenty-six hours

********Life Outside**********

242

Day one of outside.

Housing bid has gone pear shaped.

Being alive hell.

243

Francis Dixon Lodge

say I can't have therapy.

Confused I bus home

244

The weekend is here

I play pc games and think

'Is this all there is?'

245

I try to get out

where there's not lots of people...

but they're everywhere.

246

Dealing with problems

is tiring, so I just don't,

and my life gets worse.

247

The heater got fixed

but my internet has stopped.

That's how my days are

248

The noisy traffic

outside my flat at all hours.

Just there. All the time.

249

The community

psychs and doctors nod and smile,

but no new ideas.

250

January first,

I'll give it until that date

and then take my life.

251

I spend all day long

thinking about what to do...

then I do nothing.

**********Nearly Christmas***********

252

Neighbours loud music.

A friends Christmas Day invite.

Checks and balances

253

Christmas shopping blues

Enthusiasm is hard

when I'm all shopped out.

254

The writing group stops.

Cut in half by Christmas Day.

Like everything else.

***********People************

255

My lunatic friends...

Inappropriate woman,

Hitler and quiet girl

256

My saner real friends...

The Viking, the minister,

and the gaming group.

257

Most importantly

my surrogate mum and dad,

Whom I love dearly.

258

Then there's family...

Blacksmith and his fiancée,

Sleepy, and the twin.

*********Reflections*********

259

Today seems different

I don't want to kill myself,

I'm sure it'll pass.

260

I try and work out

what happens after New Year,

but I can't tell yet

261

At the bus station

it's surprisingly quiet.

I like it a lot

262

Saw a new doctor.

He's going to refer me.

So I wait some more!

263

I've had this headache,

pounding for over a month..

My 'grouchy' excuse

264

Three relaxing days

listening to Christmas music.

Ah crap, time to smile.

265

Bipolar Stacia

and me, sat in A and E

Banter and shit jokes

266

Called the council out.

Noisy neighbours at midnight.

Let's see what happen

***********2014... I Made It Then***********

267

A quiet New Year.

What does January hold

besides a meds change?

268

Aargghhh, more noise tonight.

Council and police helpless.

Triggered, there's no choice

269

The police came 'round

to stop me taking my life.

So I made them tea.

270

P.I.P. Came through.

It only took them six months.

D.W.P. shit

271

The writing group starts,

I walk The Bradgate hallways,

to meet my soul friends

272

I'm feeling spaced out.

The medication working

or my fucking head?

273

I've brought a new stick.

It has a dragon handle.

I call it Dragon.

*********Got To Survive Till Tal's Wedding*********

274

Five more weeks to go.

Survive until the wedding.

Think only of them.

275

Existential angst.

Is there a reason I'm here?

If so, what is it?

276

Staying in my flat.

Finding no reason to leave.

Hating having to.

277

Too much in my head,

but nothing moving forward.

My life is treacle.

278

It's been a good week

if you don't include the pain.

Which of course... you won't.

279

NHS bosses

listening to my long complaint.

They said they'll change things.

280

Got some benefits.

So now all I need to do

is choose... food or heat?

******** A New Flat********

281

I bid on a flat.

Council, ground floor, and I'm first.

Two days to find out.

282

At Showcase Smoothie

I learn how to breath and sing.

Maybe I'll come back.

283

I lost the flat bid.

More roller coaster bidding.

Bid, win, lose, then win.

284

Promised not to die

So how best to survive Feb?

Moving flats might help.

285

Goodbye neighbour noise

Hello buzzer door and lift

I just need to wait.

286

Advisor Debbie

helping with all the long forms,

helping me to cope.

287

It's going smoothly

which makes my anxieties

increase even more.

288

Pain, sleep and headache

getting worse because of the

medication change.

***********Moving To A New Flat**************

289

Packed everything up

nearly a week too early.

Anxiety sucks

290

I should be happy

but all I do is worry.

It's driving me nuts.

291

Council policy

makes me even angrier.

Some things never change.

292

Three days till the move.

So then my walking stick breaks.

Thank you universe

293

Moving day is good

except for the pain I'm in

from doing too much.

*******But Life Still Goes On************

294

A full calendar

of appointments and meet ups.

I just want to rest.

295

I see the paint cans

then the mess my walls are in,

And will myself on.

296

DVD's all sold

so that I can get through March,

and maybe April.

297

Spoiling for a fight,

but they sent me a new stick.

How long will it last?

***********Haiku From A MH Writing Group***********

298

Dysfunctional me.

I'm always watching and watched

by better people.

299

I'm searching my mind
I can't find the words I want,
Then what use am I?

300

I try to be me.
See that I am Yin and Yang
not good and not bad

301

The lost months gone by
then all the shouting voices
Asked me 'what went wrong'?

302

Impossible things..
The things you dare not think of
and then I was dead.

303

Wanting to not live

is a blessing and a curse,

to be and not die.

304

Watch that tune, I ask.

No more impossible than

still being alive

*************Nothing To Die For*********

305

My son gets married

so I get a new daughter.

I think we're good friends.

306

I've unpacked my stuff.

The flat needs decorating.

Things are moving on.

307

I lost my best friend

because he really messed up,

and then he dumped me!

308

Cooked a goat curry

for the alpha group at church.

Sacrificial goat.

309

Painting when I can.

The hall and kitchen are done.

Now I need to rest

310

ESA came through

two days before a letter

says no ESA!

311

A housing letter...

The rent has not yet gone through.

It's all going wrong

312

Waiting in my flat

for a parcel that is due

in two week's time. Doh.

313

'God gets the credit',

I said to the minister,

'so he gets the blame'.

314

Benefits and rent

sorted by my adviser.

What will life do next?

*****Healthy Eating?*******

315

I've been eating less,

but now I'm eating nothing.

Nine days and counting

316

Easter.. Jesus dies.

If I still believed in god

then I'd be jealous.

317

The pain has gone down

but I still don't feel happy.

I'm still not eating.

318

I feel quite content

while I'm in my cosy flat,

never going out.

319

Living on milk shakes,

smoothies for my five a day.

My 'no food' meal plan.

320

No motivation,

Can't seem to do anything,

so I just lie here.

321

My birthday was crap.

Invited for a meal out

but without my sons.

*********Social Anxiety*********

322

Facebook group 'believe'

(for people with mental health)

is my online life.

323

Mayday! Spring is here.

The sun is shining out there

but my flat is safe.

324

I only go out

for appointments or meetings.

Its safer in here.

325

Bought a radio

to make the day go faster.

It makes my head numb.

326

My amazing flat

is now all decorated

thanks to sons and friends.

327

Interestingly

suicide reasons are gone

but suicidal.

328

Most of this month (May)

I am on a Facebook group

for mental health friends.

*******Romance?*********

329

I ask someone out

and she finally said yes.

Northampton awaits.

330

Anne Julie Spencer,

a lovely person (me too).

I think she likes me.

331

Four kids and two pets!

Her home life is chaotic.

I must be insane.

332

Left home too early.

The bus doesn't take that long...

Drinking tea in Pret.

333

I must remember

to buy some flowers, Roses.

I hope she likes them.

334

She does like roses

and the date is going well.

A relaxed pub meal.

335

We both have some rules.

No kissing on the first date

is one of her rules.

336

And then she drops me!

It's her, it's not me, she says.

unsurprisingly.

337

Don't know what to do.

I don't enjoy anything.

I just want to sleep.

*******Life Goes On And On And On******

338

My meds got messed up.

No meds for forty-eight hours...

Pain and suicide?

339

GP and chemist...

Communication errors,

wrong the last five times!

340

My internet stopped,

I feel like I'm being plagued

by the universe.

341

Two days of no meds

and I can see clearly now.

Suicide is peace

*******June**********

342

June and the Fibro

Gives me a pain free-ish week

and then it came back.

343

My wrist really hurts...

No, not from masturbating

but from the Fibro.

344

My meds zone me out,

so I have almost no will

to do anything.

345

I'm spending a lot

on things I don't really need.

It's boredom spending.

346

I've started eating,

only really small amounts

when I'm out with friends

347

Everything is good...

Flat, money, friends, family,

Still suicidal!

348

An ordination

For Sami... Also called John,

I didn't know that.

349

During the sermon

I heard the funniest joke...

TA-DA said Jesus :)

350

Writing class restarts.

Met old friends and some new ones.

I still write haiku.

351

Asked Anne out again,

amused by my cheekiness

she said yes. I hope.

352

Gone back to no food.

Feels like the right thing to do.

It saves money though.

353

Mental health Haiku

Admission to post discharge

One calendar year

HAIKU FROM THE ASYLUM

ABOUT THE AUTHOR

David Rollins grew up through an emotionally and sexually abusive childhood into a screwed up father of two sons (who are doing much better than him), and has had careers in care, libraries and printing. Having had an ordinary life David had had enough and decided to take his own life. This is what happened next.

Other Authors With Green Cat Books

Lisa J Rivers –

Why I have So Many Cats

Winding Down

Searching (Coming 2018)

Luna Felis –

Life Well Lived

Gabriel Eziorobo –

Words Of My Mouth

The Brain Behind Freelance Writing

Mike Herring –

Nature Boy

Glyn Roberts & David Smith –

Prince Porrig And The Calamitous Carbuncle

(other Prince Porrig books to follow)

Peach Berry –

A Bag Of Souls

Michelle DuVal -

The Coach

Sean Gaughan –

And God For His Own

Elijah Barns –

The Witch and Jet Splinters: Part 1. A Bustle In The Hedgerow

ARE YOU A WRITER?

We are looking for writers to send in their manuscripts.

If you would like to submit your work, please send a small sample to

books@green-cat.co

GREEN CAT BOOKS

www.green-cat.co/books

Made in the USA
Columbia, SC
17 November 2017